Table of Contents

1 Introduction to API Gateways

API gateways act as a central point of control for all incoming and outgoing API requests. They sit in front of your backend services, acting as a reverse proxy and providing numerous benefits. Think of them as security guards and traffic controllers for your application's APIs, ensuring smooth and secure operation. This significantly simplifies the management of multiple microservices, eliminating the need to manage each service individually. The resulting streamlined architecture improves maintainability and reduces complexity.

Imagine trying to manage dozens of individual microservices directly. It's a logistical nightmare; a single point of failure in one service could impact your entire application. An API gateway addresses this by abstracting away the underlying complexities. It provides a unified interface, simplifying the interaction between clients and backend services, hence reducing the overall development and maintenance effort. Developers can focus on core business logic without worrying about low-level infrastructure concerns, a major boost to productivity.

The improved security offered by an API gateway is paramount. Instead of exposing each microservice directly to the public internet, which increases your attack surface significantly, the gateway acts as a shield, protecting your backend systems from unauthorized access. It centralizes security policies, allowing for consistent application of authentication, authorization, and rate limiting across all APIs. This centralized approach significantly enhances your overall security posture. By implementing robust authentication and authorization mechanisms within the gateway, you can control who accesses what, mitigating potential risks.

Furthermore, API gateways offer considerable scalability advantages. They handle the load balancing and traffic management, ensuring that requests are distributed efficiently across your backend services. This prevents overloading individual microservices, especially during peak demand. This is critical for ensuring high availability and responsiveness of your applications. Scalability is not only about handling increased traffic; it also involves efficiently managing resources, optimizing performance, and scaling down when demand decreases – all features the API gateway helps implement.

Beyond security and scalability, API gateways enhance the overall maintainability of your system. They allow for easy monitoring and logging of all API traffic. This centralized logging provides valuable insights into application usage, helping identify performance bottlenecks, security vulnerabilities, and potential areas for improvement. The ability to quickly identify and address these issues is invaluable in ensuring your application's health and stability, thus preventing service disruptions and improving customer experience. This data-driven approach allows you to proactively manage your API infrastructure, making it easier to adapt to future changes.

Implementing an API gateway is not just a matter of deploying software; it requires careful planning and consideration of your specific needs and architecture. Understanding your existing infrastructure, the capabilities of different gateway solutions, and the potential challenges are crucial for successful implementation. Careful planning ensures the best fit for your application's requirements and prevents costly mistakes down the line. Choosing the right gateway depends on factors like scalability requirements, security needs, and existing infrastructure.

Proper configuration is essential to unlock the full potential of an API gateway. You need to configure authentication and authorization mechanisms, define routes, implement rate limiting policies, and set up monitoring and logging. Without proper configuration, the gateway might not function as intended and could even introduce security vulnerabilities. This includes configuring things like security headers, input validation, and custom authentication flows, depending on the specifics of the architecture and application. Remember the gateway is only as effective as its configuration allows.

Finally, integrating an API gateway into your existing infrastructure requires careful planning and execution. The implementation process should be iterative, allowing for adjustments based on your experience and feedback. A phased rollout allows you to assess and address potential issues before scaling up to a full deployment. This phased approach minimizes disruption to your operational environment and enables thorough testing. Continuous monitoring after deployment is essential to track performance and proactively address any issues that arise. This iterative process ensures a smooth and successful integration.

1.1 What are API Gateways?

An API gateway acts as a central point of control for all requests to your backend services. Imagine it as a sophisticated receptionist for your microservices, meticulously managing and filtering every incoming request before forwarding it to the appropriate service. This centralized approach simplifies the management of multiple APIs, providing a single entry point for all client applications. Instead of clients connecting directly to individual microservices, potentially exposing vulnerabilities and complicating management, they interact solely with the gateway, which then handles routing, authentication, and other crucial tasks.

This single point of contact allows for easier implementation of cross-cutting concerns, such as security, logging, and rate limiting. Implementing these features across numerous microservices individually would be a logistical nightmare, a repetitive and time-consuming process riddled with the possibility of inconsistencies and security gaps. The gateway, however, allows you to handle these concerns in one location, ensuring uniformity and efficiency. This centralized management is a significant advantage, particularly when managing a large number of microservices.

Think of it like a high-traffic website: you wouldn't want every visitor to directly access the server hosting individual pages; the load would be unmanageable and the system would quickly become unstable. An API gateway is similar; it acts as a reverse proxy, efficiently managing the load distribution across the microservices. This intelligent load balancing ensures that no single service becomes overwhelmed, enhancing the overall stability and resilience of your system. It can also handle scaling dynamically, adjusting to traffic fluctuations automatically.

Beyond load balancing, an API gateway offers crucial security benefits. It acts as a security perimeter, shielding your backend services from direct exposure to the outside world. This is particularly important in a microservices architecture, where each service might have its own vulnerabilities. The gateway can enforce authentication and authorization policies, ensuring that only authorized clients can access specific services. This centralized security layer allows for consistent application of security measures, removing the risk of inconsistencies across individual services. It simplifies the maintenance and updates of security protocols, significantly reducing your exposure to various cyber threats.

Further, API gateways facilitate easier management of API versions. As your microservices evolve, you'll likely introduce new versions of your APIs. The gateway can seamlessly manage these different versions, ensuring backward compatibility with older clients while supporting new functionalities. This controlled versioning is vital for maintaining stability while simultaneously upgrading the functionality of your application. Without a gateway, managing multiple versions directly across numerous microservices could lead to significant complications and potential conflicts.

Moreover, an API gateway helps in implementing sophisticated traffic management strategies. This includes routing requests to specific instances of a microservice based on various factors, such as geographical location or load. Furthermore, it enables features such as A/B testing, allowing you to deploy new API versions alongside existing ones, gradually rolling out new functionalities and monitoring their performance before a full-scale deployment. This careful rollout procedure helps to minimize disruptions and allows for continuous monitoring and improvement.

In summary, an API gateway is more than just a simple intermediary; it is a vital component in a modern microservices architecture. It provides a range of benefits, from simplified management and enhanced security to improved scalability and performance. Its functionality is essential for the efficient and secure operation of any microservice-based application. By centralizing key functionalities and improving manageability, it allows developers to focus on building and improving their services, rather than dealing with the complexities of infrastructure management and security. Therefore, understanding and utilizing its potential is critical for success in the modern world of microservices. Choosing the right API gateway solution is crucial; research and careful consideration of various solutions should always be prioritized to find the one that perfectly aligns with the specific demands and structure of your application.

1.2 Benefits of API Gateways

Centralizing API management offers significant advantages. An API gateway acts as a single point of contact for all client requests, simplifying management and reducing the complexity of directly exposing numerous microservices. This streamlined approach improves maintainability and reduces the overhead associated with managing individual service endpoints. Updates and changes can be implemented centrally, impacting all clients simultaneously, streamlining the deployment process significantly.

Consider the enhanced security an API gateway provides. It acts as a robust security layer, shielding your backend microservices from direct exposure to potential threats. This protection includes implementing authentication mechanisms, enforcing rate limiting, and validating inputs – all before requests even reach your sensitive services. By centralizing these security measures, you significantly reduce the attack surface and maintain a consistent security posture across your API landscape. This is far more efficient than implementing individual security measures within each microservice.

Improved scalability is another key benefit. The API gateway can handle increased traffic loads, distributing requests efficiently across your microservices. This prevents individual services from being overloaded and ensures consistent performance, even during peak demand. This load balancing capability allows for easier horizontal scaling—adding more gateway instances as needed, rather than scaling every microservice individually. This flexible architecture ensures your system can adapt to changing demands without compromising performance or stability.

Furthermore, API gateways facilitate easier monitoring and analytics. They provide a central point for collecting metrics and logs, offering valuable insights into API usage patterns and potential problems. This centralized data collection simplifies performance monitoring, debugging, and identifying security vulnerabilities. Understanding usage patterns and performance bottlenecks enables proactive optimization and ensures a seamless user experience. Real-time monitoring allows for immediate intervention in case of an issue, minimizing disruption to service.

Finally, API gateways enhance the developer experience. They provide well-defined interfaces and consistent documentation, simplifying integration for clients. This improves collaboration between development teams and empowers developers to build and deploy applications faster, leading to shorter development cycles and quicker time-to-market. Consistent API documentation, provided by the gateway, ensures smooth interactions between client and server-side applications regardless of the complexity of the backend architecture. This removes a significant barrier to entry for developers interacting with your API ecosystem.

The benefits extend beyond simple functionality. The abstraction layer provided by the gateway allows for easier migration and refactoring of microservices without impacting clients directly. This simplifies ongoing maintenance and development, enabling your system to remain adaptable to changing requirements and technological advancements. With a gateway in place, internal architectural changes can occur without clients needing updates, preserving their stability and simplifying updates.

In essence, implementing an API gateway is about more than just security and scalability; it's about building a more robust, efficient, and maintainable API landscape. The centralization, security features, and improved developer experience lead to a more stable, resilient, and adaptable system that easily scales to meet changing demands. By providing a single entry point, the gateway simplifies management, improves security, and ultimately leads to a more efficient development lifecycle. Choosing to implement an API gateway, therefore, isn't merely a choice; it's a strategic decision that yields significant long-term benefits for any organization managing multiple microservices and a complex API ecosystem. This holistic approach translates to considerable cost savings in the long run, due to increased efficiency and reduced operational overhead. The improved scalability directly translates into savings on infrastructure, as resources are managed more efficiently. Furthermore, the reduced development time and enhanced developer experience contribute to lower labor costs. In summary, the benefits extend well beyond immediate gains, offering a valuable long-term return on investment.

2 Authentication Fundamentals

Understanding authentication is paramount when securing your microservices. It's the bedrock upon which all your security measures are built. Without robust authentication, your API gateway is essentially a wide-open door, inviting unauthorized access and potential breaches. Think of it like the key to your house – without a strong, secure key, anyone can simply walk in.

OAuth 2.0 is a widely adopted authorization framework, not an authentication protocol. This distinction is crucial. OAuth 2.0 focuses on granting access to protected resources, not verifying the user's identity. The actual authentication – verifying who the user is – happens separately. For instance, a user might authenticate through a social login like Google or Facebook, then use OAuth 2.0 to authorize access to specific data within your application. This framework provides several grant types – Authorization Code, Implicit, Resource Owner Password Credentials, and Client Credentials – each suited to different scenarios and levels of security. Choosing the right grant type is crucial for optimal security. Incorrect usage can lead to vulnerabilities and compromised access.

OpenID Connect (OIDC) builds on top of OAuth 2.0, adding a layer of identity verification. Where OAuth 2.0 primarily deals with authorization, OIDC provides a standardized way for a client to verify the identity of a user and obtain basic profile information. This means you're not just granting access, you're also confirming who is requesting it. This extra layer offers enhanced security and simplifies the authentication process. Implementing OIDC frequently involves the use of JSON Web Tokens (JWTs).

JSON Web Tokens, or JWTs, are a compact and self-contained way to represent claims securely between parties. Essentially, a JWT is a digital token containing information about the user, encoded using JSON and signed with a digital signature. This signature ensures the token's integrity and authenticity. Verifying a JWT is a relatively straightforward process, involving checking the signature and ensuring the token hasn't expired. JWTs are commonly used in conjunction with OAuth 2.0 and OIDC flows, providing a standardized and efficient way to pass authentication and authorization information between the client, the authorization server, and the resource server. The compact nature of JWTs makes them suitable for use in microservices environments, ensuring efficient and secure communication.

The selection and implementation of these protocols are critical to overall security. Consider the sensitivity of your data and choose the protocols and grant types that best address your specific security needs. Don't simply pick the "easiest" option; select the approach that delivers the strongest security posture while remaining efficient for your system and users. This may involve understanding the trade-offs associated with different grant types, such as the security implications of using the Resource Owner Password Credentials grant. Thorough planning and understanding of the nuances of each protocol are absolutely necessary. Failure to do so can open the door to security breaches that compromise user data and the integrity of your microservices. Improper handling of secrets involved in JWT generation or the storage of client secrets can also lead to vulnerabilities. Remember, the best security is a layered approach, using a combination of authentication methods and security best practices to achieve comprehensive protection. This is a continual learning process, and staying up to date with best practices is vital for maintaining a strong security posture. Constant vigilance and continuous refinement of your authentication mechanisms are key to securing your system against evolving threats and attack vectors. Carefully consider all aspects of your implementation, from the selection of grant types to the securing of your tokens and associated cryptographic keys.

2.1 OAuth 2.0 Explained

OAuth 2.0 is an authorization framework, not an authentication protocol. This crucial distinction means it doesn't verify who a user is, but rather what they are allowed to do. Think of it as granting a specific permission, like accessing a protected resource, rather than confirming identity. Authentication, conversely, is the process of verifying a user's identity. Therefore, OAuth 2.0 often works in conjunction with other methods to create a complete security solution. This collaborative approach strengthens the overall security posture of your system. Understanding this fundamental difference prevents confusion and enables you to properly integrate it into your API gateway.

Unlike simpler authorization mechanisms, OAuth 2.0's strength lies in its flexibility. It offers various "grant types," each suited for different scenarios. The Authorization Code Grant, for example, is ideal for web applications, prioritizing security by exchanging an authorization code for an access token on the server-side. This prevents your client's secrets from being exposed directly. The Implicit Grant, on the other hand, is simpler, directly providing an access token to the client, but it's less secure and generally suitable for less sensitive applications. Choosing the right grant type is pivotal for balancing security and ease of implementation. A well-considered choice significantly impacts your application's robustness and user experience.

The Resource Owner Password Credentials Grant, while seemingly convenient, warrants extra caution. It requires the client to directly request an access token using the user's credentials. This approach is risky unless you can guarantee the client's security, making it generally less favored due to the heightened risk of credential compromise. Client Credentials Grant is another option, suitable for machine-to-machine communication. In this type of authentication, the client presents its own credentials, not a user's, making it appropriate for background processes. Finally, Refresh Tokens are crucial for extending the lifetime of access tokens, allowing for continued access without repeated authentication requests. These tokens need careful management to prevent abuse and potential security breaches.

Implementing OAuth 2.0 involves a carefully orchestrated flow. The client initiates the process by requesting authorization from the authorization server. This server then prompts the resource owner (the user) to grant permission. If the user approves, the authorization server returns an authorization code (or an access token, depending on the grant type). The client then exchanges this code for an access token, which grants access to the protected resources. Each step needs meticulous attention to detail. This entire process, from initial request to final access token, forms the backbone of secure API interaction. You must understand each stage and potential vulnerabilities.

Consider the role of the access token. This token serves as proof of authorization for accessing protected resources. It's typically short-lived, enhancing security. Upon expiry, the refresh token can be used to obtain a new

one, ensuring continuous access without requiring the user to repeatedly authenticate. However, the refresh token itself should be well-protected, employing robust measures against theft or misuse. Its security is directly related to the security of your whole system. A compromise here compromises your entire system.
Integrating OAuth 2.0 with your API gateway requires careful planning and consideration of your specific needs. You might leverage existing identity providers or build a custom solution. The choice depends on factors such as your scale, security requirements, and existing infrastructure. However, regardless of your approach, remember that consistent attention to security best practices is paramount. This includes proper token handling, secure storage of secrets, and regular security audits. Regularly review your security practices and adapt to evolving threats.
Remember, security isn't a one-time fix but an ongoing process. Regular updates, audits, and a proactive security posture are critical for maintaining the integrity and security of your API gateway and the sensitive data it protects. Always stay updated on the latest security recommendations and vulnerabilities. Proper implementation minimizes the risk of exploitation and unauthorized access. Through careful consideration and implementation of these guidelines, your API gateway can benefit fully from OAuth 2.0's security features. By understanding this framework's nuances, you effectively secure your microservices and maintain user trust.

2.2 OpenID Connect Deep Dive

OpenID Connect, often abbreviated as OIDC, builds upon the OAuth 2.0 framework, adding a crucial layer for identity verification. While OAuth 2.0 focuses on granting access tokens, OIDC provides a standardized way to obtain user identity information, enhancing security and simplifying the authentication process. This is achieved through the use of ID tokens, which are JWTs containing claims about the authenticated user, such as their unique identifier, name, and email address. This robust approach minimizes the need for additional API calls to fetch user details, streamlining the authentication flow and improving overall performance.

Unlike OAuth 2.0, which primarily focuses on authorization, OIDC goes a step further by explicitly defining how to verify the identity of the user. It introduces a standardized protocol for identity providers (IdPs) to issue ID tokens, containing verifiable assertions about the user. This standardized approach facilitates interoperability between different systems and reduces the complexity of integrating with diverse identity providers. The process ensures that the access token is associated with a verified identity, drastically enhancing security and reducing the risk of unauthorized access. This is crucial for applications demanding strong identity verification, such as banking or healthcare systems.

Implementing OIDC typically involves a well-defined flow between the client application, the authorization server (often part of an API gateway), and the IdP. The client initiates the authentication process, redirecting the user to the IdP's login page. Upon successful authentication, the IdP redirects the user back to the client, providing an authorization code. The client then exchanges this code for an access token and an ID token at the authorization server. The ID token, a self-contained JWT, can be directly verified by the client, allowing secure access to the user's identity information. This eliminates the need for separate calls to profile endpoints, significantly increasing efficiency and security.

Consider a scenario where a mobile banking app uses OIDC for authentication. The user launches the app and attempts to access their account.

The app initiates the OIDC flow, sending the user to the bank's IdP for authentication. After successful login, the IdP provides the app with an access token and an ID token. The app verifies the ID token's signature and extracts the user's information, such as their account number and name, from the token's claims. This information is then used to personalize the user experience and securely access their banking details, without needing further requests to the bank's systems. The entire process is secured by using HTTPS throughout the authentication and authorization steps.

The verification of the ID token is paramount in ensuring the integrity of the authentication process. The client app verifies the token's signature using the IdP's public key, ensuring that the token originates from a trusted source and has not been tampered with. Additionally, the client validates the token's claims, ensuring that they are consistent with the expected values and haven't been altered during transmission. This dual verification process greatly minimizes the risk of man-in-the-middle attacks and ensures that the identity information is reliable and trustworthy. The detailed specifications and best practices for OIDC implementation are available in the official OIDC specification document.

Beyond basic identity verification, OIDC supports various features that enhance its capabilities and adaptability. For instance, it offers support for different response modes, allowing developers to customize how the ID and access tokens are delivered to the client application. This flexibility enables developers to accommodate various client architectures and security constraints. Furthermore, OIDC extensions allow developers to add custom claims to the ID token, enriching the information available about the authenticated user without compromising the core functionalities of OIDC. Understanding these extensions and customizing them accordingly is critical for optimizing the implementation and ensuring a tailored solution. The ability to incorporate these optional elements enhances flexibility and provides a mechanism to accommodate the unique requirements of each application.

Choosing the correct OIDC flow is crucial for ensuring optimal security and usability. The authorization code flow is generally recommended for its enhanced security, as it exchanges an authorization code for an access token and an ID token on the backend, reducing the risk of exposing sensitive information in the client. However, the implicit flow offers a simpler approach, especially for browser-based applications, but it requires careful consideration of its security implications. Selecting the appropriate flow involves understanding the trade-offs between security and implementation complexity, tailored to the specific context and security requirements of the application being built. Therefore, careful analysis and understanding of these nuances are vital. Consult the OIDC specification for further details on various flows and their specific characteristics.

In conclusion, OpenID Connect provides a robust and secure mechanism for verifying user identities in the context of OAuth 2.0. Its standardized approach simplifies the integration with identity providers, enhances security through the use of ID tokens and their verification, and offers flexibility through various flows and extensions. Understanding these aspects is crucial for building secure and efficient applications that leverage the power of OIDC for authentication. By carefully considering the various aspects outlined above, developers can effectively utilize OIDC to significantly improve their application's security posture and user experience. Mastering OIDC is therefore a significant step towards building secure and user-friendly applications within a microservices architecture.

2.3 JWT: JSON Web Tokens

JSON Web Tokens (JWTs) are a compact and self-contained way to transmit information securely between parties as a JSON object. Imagine it as a digitally signed passport, carrying all the necessary details for identification and authorization. Unlike session-based authentication, which requires constant server-side lookups, JWTs are stateless, meaning the server doesn't need to store any user-specific information during the authentication process. This significantly improves scalability and performance, a critical aspect for any microservices architecture.

JWTs follow a specific structure, consisting of three parts separated by dots: the header, the payload, and the signature. The header typically contains information about the token type and signing algorithm used. The payload holds the actual claims—data about the user—like their unique identifier, roles, and expiration time. The signature ensures the integrity and authenticity of the token, preventing tampering. It's generated using a secret key known only to the issuer and the verifier. This cryptographic signature prevents unauthorized modifications. This simple, yet robust, structure underpins their widespread adoption.

Creating a JWT involves several steps. First, you need to define the claims you want to include in the payload. These claims should be carefully chosen, only including data strictly necessary for authorization. Overloading the JWT with unnecessary data can lead to security vulnerabilities and performance issues. The header also needs specification, typically specifying the alg (algorithm) and typ (type). Once the header and payload are ready, they're encoded using Base64Url. Finally, the signature is generated using the chosen algorithm and a secret key. This complete encoded JWT string can then be passed to the client.

Verifying a JWT is equally important. The receiving party needs to decode the token, verify the signature using the same secret key used during creation, and validate the claims. This verification process ensures that the token hasn't been tampered with and that the claims are still valid. Failure at any stage means the token should be rejected. Libraries for most common programming languages greatly simplify both creation and verification, minimizing the risk of errors and ensuring a standardized process. Consistent, precise, and thoroughly tested validation is paramount.

Security considerations are crucial when working with JWTs. Never embed sensitive information directly into the payload. Instead, use the JWT to identify the user, then retrieve sensitive data from a secure backend using that identification. Protect your secret keys diligently. A compromised secret key grants an attacker complete control over your system. Employ a robust key management system, rotate keys regularly, and store them securely, preferably using dedicated secrets management tools. Remember, the security of your application hinges on the security of your keys.

One common misconception involves storing the entire JWT within a browser's local storage or cookie. While convenient, this practice increases the risk of exposing sensitive information to cross-site scripting attacks. A more secure approach is to store a short-lived, refresh token on the client-side, and use it to regularly obtain new JWTs. This mitigates the risk of compromised tokens impacting a long duration. Using secure HTTP-only cookies for refresh tokens further enhances the protection against cross-site scripting vulnerabilities. This multi-layered security approach adds significant strength.

In integration with API gateways, JWTs play a central role in securing access to your microservices. The gateway can be configured to accept JWTs as authentication tokens, validating them against the issuer's secret key before routing requests to the appropriate microservice. This offloads authentication logic from individual microservices, making them simpler and more maintainable. Efficient integration of JWTs into your gateway simplifies architecture, making it more robust. Furthermore, the gateway can enforce additional security policies, such as rate limiting and request validation.

Consider different approaches to handling JWTs depending on your specific needs. For instance, you might opt for a short-lived JWT for authentication and a longer-lived refresh token for maintaining the session. Carefully choose your signing algorithm, considering factors like security and performance. The choice of algorithm also directly affects compatibility with different systems and libraries. These are crucial elements in building a comprehensive authentication system. Always remember to balance security and user experience; overly restrictive measures can frustrate legitimate users.

Ultimately, integrating JWTs into your API gateway strategy offers a powerful method for authentication and authorization. Their stateless nature improves scalability, while their built-in security features offer a strong defense against many common threats. By carefully managing your keys and understanding the security implications, you can build a robust and efficient system. Thorough testing and regular security audits are essential for maintaining the integrity and security of your system over time. Regularly review your security practices and adapt them to the latest threats. Using JWTs effectively requires a considered, holistic approach that balances security, performance, and ease of use.

3 API Gateway Security Best Practices

Robust security is paramount. Neglecting it invites vulnerabilities, potentially exposing sensitive data and disrupting services. Implementing strong security measures isn't merely a checklist; it's a continuous process requiring vigilance and adaptation. Think of your API gateway as the castle gate, carefully controlled access is key.

Rate limiting and throttling are your first line of defense. They prevent malicious actors from overwhelming your system with excessive requests, a common tactic in denial-of-service attacks. Configure your gateway to limit the number of requests per unit of time from a single IP address or API key. Dynamically adjust these limits based on real-time traffic patterns, allowing legitimate users smooth access while thwarting abusers. Consider using a sliding window approach for more accurate rate limiting. Implement different rate limits based on various factors like user roles and request type for a granular control.

Input validation is crucial. Never trust user-provided data. Always validate and sanitize all inputs before processing them. This prevents injection attacks such as SQL injection, cross-site scripting (XSS), and command injection, all of which can compromise your system's integrity. Use input validation libraries and regular expressions to enforce data types, lengths, and formats. Sanitize user inputs to prevent malicious code insertion, removing or escaping potentially harmful characters. Remember to validate data at multiple layers of your application, not just the API gateway, creating a defense-in-depth strategy.

Security headers are your unsung heroes. Employ HTTP Strict Transport Security (HSTS) to enforce HTTPS connections, preventing man-in-the-middle attacks. Use Content Security Policy (CSP) to control the resources the browser loads, mitigating XSS risks. Other vital headers include X-Frame-Options to prevent clickjacking and X-Content-Type-Options to prevent MIME-sniffing vulnerabilities. Regularly review and update the security headers, keeping up with the latest best practices. Detailed documentation is essential for ensuring all the security headers and their configurations are clearly understood by the development team.

API key management deserves meticulous attention. Use strong, randomly generated keys and implement secure key rotation procedures. Avoid hard-coding keys in your application code. Use a robust key management system for storage and retrieval, implementing access control measures to limit who can access and use those keys. Implement key revocation mechanisms to immediately disable compromised keys. For enhanced security, consider using short-lived access tokens.

Monitoring and logging are indispensable. Track all API requests, including successful and failed attempts, along with timestamps and other relevant details. Use a centralized logging system for easier analysis. Set up alerts for unusual activity, such as sudden spikes in requests or failed authentication attempts. Regularly review your logs to detect and respond to potential security threats and performance issues. Ensure that your logging system is capable of scaling with your traffic volume and incorporates features like real-time analysis and anomaly detection. Regularly review and refine your logging strategy to meet your organization's evolving security and performance needs.

Effective API gateway security requires a layered approach. It's not just about configuring individual features; it's about understanding how they work together. Consistent monitoring, regular security audits, and proactive updates ensure the ongoing integrity of your API gateway. It's an iterative process, demanding continual refinement and vigilance. Remember, security isn't a destination, but an ongoing journey, demanding both expertise and constant attention. The ultimate goal is to balance the need for robust security with ease of use and performance. A well-secured API gateway is not a barrier to access, but a responsible guardian of your valuable data and services.

3.1 Rate Limiting and Throttling

Rate limiting and throttling are crucial security measures within an API gateway, acting as the first line of defense against various attacks. They prevent malicious actors from overwhelming your system with excessive requests, ensuring service availability for legitimate users. Think of it like a bouncer at a nightclub – they control the flow of people, preventing overcrowding and maintaining order. Without these mechanisms, your APIs become vulnerable to denial-of-service (DoS) attacks, where a flood of requests renders your services unresponsive. Implementing effective rate limiting and throttling policies is paramount for maintaining the integrity and stability of your microservices architecture.

The fundamental principle behind rate limiting is to restrict the number of requests a client can make within a specified time window. This window can be configured in various ways, using factors such as the IP address of the client, API key, or even user identity. For example, you might limit a specific IP address to 100 requests per minute or an API key to 1000 requests per hour. Exceeding these limits triggers actions like temporarily blocking the client or returning an error message, preventing further requests from being processed. The granular control is what makes this incredibly useful. Throttling, a more sophisticated approach, builds upon rate limiting by dynamically adjusting request limits based on system resources. It continuously monitors the server load and adjusts the rate limits accordingly. If the server is under heavy load, the throttling mechanism reduces the number of requests being processed to prevent overload. Conversely, if the server has sufficient capacity, the limits are relaxed, optimizing resource utilization and throughput. This dynamic approach is far more adaptable than a simple static limit that is set and forgotten. You may have heard the term "circuit breaker" in software development. Throttling shares some similarities, but it focuses more on prevention than reacting to failures.

Choosing the right approach depends greatly on your specific needs and the complexity of your system. For simpler applications, basic rate limiting might suffice. However, for complex systems with fluctuating loads and many users, a dynamic throttling strategy proves far more robust and efficient. Consider your architecture and the expected traffic patterns; a well-designed system may use a combination of both, offering a layered defense.

Implementing rate limiting and throttling often involves using specialized tools or features provided by your API gateway. Many modern gateways offer built-in mechanisms to configure rate limits and integrate with monitoring systems, making the implementation relatively straightforward. However, for enhanced control and customization, you might need to write custom code or integrate third-party libraries. Remember to thoroughly test your implementation to ensure that it effectively protects your system without unduly impacting legitimate users. Testing should include both normal usage scenarios and simulated attacks to gauge the system's resilience.

Accurate monitoring and logging are crucial for evaluating the effectiveness of your rate-limiting and throttling policies. The data collected provides valuable insights into the frequency and patterns of requests, allowing you to fine-tune your policies over time. Monitoring helps spot potential issues before they escalate into full-blown attacks. It's easy to fall into the trap of implementing a system and then ignoring it, but continuous improvement is vital. Regular analysis allows for better adjustments based on trends that may develop, further securing your system's stability. By constantly analyzing these logs you can further refine and optimize the system. It is an iterative process, and only through careful observation will you understand and improve this critical aspect of your API security.

Effective rate limiting and throttling are not just about preventing attacks; they're about resource management and system stability. They are indispensable for ensuring the long-term health of your API and the satisfaction of your users. By carefully considering your needs and implementation strategy, you can build a robust defense against a wide variety of threats. Never underestimate the impact of proactive security measures. The time spent implementing and managing them is an investment in the future of your system. Implementing this, along with the other suggestions detailed in this book will provide your system with the best possible protection. So take the time to do it properly, and you'll be well-rewarded.

3.2 Input Validation and Sanitization

Protecting your API gateway from malicious input is paramount. Failing to validate and sanitize user input leaves your system vulnerable to a range of attacks, from simple data corruption to devastating SQL injection and cross-site scripting (XSS) vulnerabilities. These attacks can compromise sensitive data, disrupt service availability, and even grant unauthorized access to your entire system. Therefore, robust input validation and sanitization are non-negotiable aspects of secure API design.

Consider a scenario where a user attempts to submit data exceeding the expected length or containing unexpected characters. Without proper validation, this could lead to buffer overflows, potentially crashing your application or creating pathways for attackers to inject malicious code. Similarly, if your API accepts user-supplied SQL queries without proper sanitization, a malicious actor could craft queries to access or modify sensitive data beyond their intended access rights, leading to significant data breaches. These are not hypothetical threats; they are common vulnerabilities exploited in real-world attacks daily.

The first line of defense is rigorous input validation. This involves checking that the data received conforms to predefined rules and constraints. For example, you might check that a user's email address adheres to a specific format, a phone number is the correct length, or a date is within a valid range. Employing strong typing, specifying data lengths, and using regular expressions are crucial techniques. Remember, expecting the unexpected is key; carefully consider all potential inputs, even those seemingly unlikely. Never assume the user will always provide data in the expected format. Build your validation rules based on a solid understanding of the data types and constraints, not assumptions.

Beyond validation, sanitization is equally critical. Sanitization is the process of removing or modifying potentially harmful characters from user-supplied data before it's used within your application. For instance, removing HTML tags from user input prevents XSS attacks, while escaping special characters prevents SQL injection. Choosing the right sanitization techniques depends on the context. A common approach is to escape special characters based on the target context. For instance, escaping characters differently for SQL queries, HTML output, and command-line arguments.

Implementing comprehensive input validation and sanitization requires a multi-layered approach. Begin by defining clear validation rules for each input field at the API design stage itself. Utilize your chosen programming language's built-in validation tools to automatically enforce basic rules. For more complex validation, leverage external libraries or frameworks specifically designed for input validation. These frameworks often provide pre-built validation rules and convenient mechanisms for integrating validation into your API's request handling pipeline.

Consider using a consistent approach across your APIs. Establishing a standardized way to handle input validation and sanitization ensures consistency, improving maintainability and reducing the risk of overlooking vulnerabilities. Centralizing your validation and sanitization logic in reusable components also facilitates easier updates and maintenance. Moreover, thoroughly document your validation and sanitization rules to ensure consistency within your team and allow for easier debugging and maintenance. Regularly review and update your validation and sanitization rules as your API evolves. As your application grows and changes, so will the types and forms of data being processed, and your existing rules may no longer be sufficient. Keeping your validation and sanitization strategies up-to-date is an ongoing process and a crucial aspect of maintaining API security. Conduct regular security audits and penetration testing to identify weaknesses in your input handling procedures. These audits can reveal vulnerabilities not detected through routine testing.

Remember, input validation and sanitization are not mutually exclusive; they are complementary safeguards working in tandem to protect your API. Input validation prevents many issues before they can even occur, preventing potentially malicious data from being processed. Sanitization cleanses data that has passed initial validation, eliminating any remaining potential threats. Effective input validation and sanitization require meticulous planning and proactive security measures. By carefully planning and implementing these strategies, you can substantially reduce your API's vulnerability to a wide array of attacks. The extra effort translates directly into a more secure and robust application, safeguarding your data and your users' trust.

3.3 Security Headers and Protocols

Deploying HTTPS is paramount. It's the bedrock of secure communication, encrypting data exchanged between the client and your API gateway. Without it, sensitive information is exposed to interception. Ensure you obtain and properly configure an SSL/TLS certificate from a trusted Certificate Authority (CA). Regular renewal is crucial; a lapsed certificate renders your HTTPS protection useless, leaving your API vulnerable. Consider using a robust Certificate Management System (CMS) to automate the renewal process and prevent outages. Proper configuration includes enabling HTTP Strict Transport Security (HSTS) to enforce HTTPS connections and prevent downgrade attacks. Implement perfect forward secrecy (PFS) to protect against future compromises of your private keys, ensuring ongoing session security. Monitor for certificate validity and expiration, addressing issues promptly to avoid disruptions and security breaches.

Content Security Policy (CSP) is your shield against cross-site scripting (XSS) attacks. By explicitly defining the sources from which your API is permitted to load resources, you significantly reduce the risk of malicious code injection. A carefully crafted CSP header dictates allowed sources for scripts, styles, images, and other assets. Regular updates to this policy are essential to adapt to evolving threats and your application's changing needs. Thoroughly test your CSP implementation, verifying that it doesn't inadvertently block legitimate resources. Incorrectly configured CSP can lead to broken functionality and a diminished user experience. Remember that rigorous testing is vital to ensure that your CSP protects against attacks without unduly hindering your API's functionality.

The HTTP Strict Transport Security (HSTS) header is more than just a simple security enhancement; it's a proactive measure to prevent man-in-the-middle attacks. By instructing browsers to always connect to your API using HTTPS, you eliminate the possibility of an attacker forcing an insecure HTTP connection. This header, once set, compels browsers to refuse all insecure connections, effectively hardening your API against downgrade attacks. Implement HSTS with a preload list submission for maximum browser compliance. However, understand that HSTS is a permanent commitment, demanding careful planning to avoid disruptions if you mistakenly configure it. Moreover, ensure your certificate is properly provisioned before deploying HSTS to prevent outages and errors. Implementing HSTS is a strategic choice that, when implemented correctly, dramatically boosts your API's security posture.

X-Frame-Options is a less widely discussed but equally crucial header. This header controls whether your API can be embedded in an iframe, helping to mitigate clickjacking attacks. By setting the X-Frame-Options header appropriately, you prevent malicious websites from embedding your API within their own pages, deceiving users into interacting with fraudulent content. Choose the most restrictive option that aligns with your API's intended usage – denying embedding altogether ("DENY") is generally recommended unless specific circumstances warrant a more lenient approach ("SAMEORIGIN"). This simple yet effective measure contributes significantly to your API's overall security, preventing unauthorized access and enhancing the protection of your users' interactions.

Reflected XSS attacks can be mitigated using the X-XSS-Protection header. This header informs the browser whether to enable its built-in XSS filtering mechanism. While not a replacement for robust server-side input validation, it provides an additional layer of protection against XSS vulnerabilities. Setting this header correctly ensures that your browser leverages its built-in defenses, thus minimizing the impact of reflected XSS attacks. The decision to enable this header relies on the evaluation of the browser's filtering capabilities versus the potential disruption or incompatibility. Always consider the potential trade-offs and test thoroughly to ensure optimal protection without compromising your API's operation.

Implementing these security headers is not just about checking boxes; it's a fundamental step towards building a robust and secure API gateway. Each header serves a specific purpose, contributing to a layered security approach. The combination of these headers, together with proper server-side validation and other security practices, creates a significantly stronger defense against common web vulnerabilities. Regular reviews and updates of your security headers are essential, as new vulnerabilities and attack vectors constantly emerge. Consider integrating automated security testing into your development lifecycle to ensure the effectiveness of your security measures. Proactive security is an ongoing process; continuous vigilance and adaptation are vital to maintaining a secure API gateway.

3.4 API Key Management

Effective API key management is paramount for securing your APIs. Think of API keys as digital keys to your application's resources; losing control of them is akin to handing out your house keys to strangers. Robust management prevents unauthorized access, protects sensitive data, and ensures the overall integrity of your system. Neglecting this crucial aspect can lead to significant security breaches and reputational damage. Proactive measures are vital, not simply reactive responses to incidents.

Implementing a strong API key management strategy requires a multifaceted approach. It begins with the generation process itself. Keys should be generated using cryptographically secure random number generators to eliminate predictability and resist brute-force attacks. Avoid simple sequential numbering; the randomness adds an essential layer of protection. Length is also critical, aiming for a significant number of characters to drastically increase the difficulty of guessing.

Regular key rotation is a fundamental best practice. Similar to changing your passwords periodically, rotating API keys limits the impact of compromised keys. Establish a clear rotation schedule based on risk assessment and the sensitivity of the data accessed through the API. This ensures that even if a key is exposed, its window of vulnerability is drastically reduced. A well-defined process ensures seamless transitions without disrupting application functionality. Automate this process whenever possible, minimizing the risk of human error and ensuring consistency.

Secure storage of API keys is just as vital as their generation and rotation. Never hardcode keys directly into your application's code. This is a significant security risk. Instead, utilize secure configuration management systems or dedicated secrets management services that provide encryption and access controls. These systems offer centralized storage, allowing for easier management, auditing, and key revocation. Implementing multi-factor authentication for access to these systems adds an additional layer of protection. Think of these systems as vaults, safeguarding your valuable keys.

Beyond secure storage, effective revocation mechanisms are essential. The ability to quickly and efficiently disable compromised or outdated keys is critical for mitigating potential damage. Implement a system that allows immediate revocation without requiring code changes or extensive downtime. This can involve listing revoked keys, blacklisting them in your gateway, or utilizing a more sophisticated system that dynamically verifies key validity. A swift response is essential to minimize damage.

Monitoring and logging activity associated with API keys offer valuable insights into usage patterns and potential security threats. Track successful and failed authentication attempts, noting timestamps and IP addresses. Establish thresholds for suspicious activities, triggering alerts to security teams when unusual patterns emerge. This proactive monitoring allows for early detection of potential attacks or misuse, paving the way for a swift response before any significant damage occurs. Careful analysis of this data can identify weaknesses and enhance security measures. Remember, effective security isn't just about preventing intrusion, it's about detecting issues promptly and responding accordingly.

Finally, educating your developers on secure API key handling practices is crucial. Provide clear guidelines on generating, storing, and using API keys securely. Promote the use of secure coding practices, emphasizing the importance of never exposing keys in publicly accessible areas such as Git repositories. Regular training and awareness sessions reinforce the importance of secure key management and help prevent accidental leaks or misuse. Consider implementing regular security audits to ensure that these best practices are being followed. Ultimately, a collaborative and knowledgeable team is the strongest defense against API key related vulnerabilities. Through careful planning and the implementation of robust systems, you can create a secure and well-protected API environment.

3.5 Monitoring and Logging

Effective monitoring and logging are paramount for maintaining the security and reliability of your API gateway. Without robust logging, identifying and resolving security breaches or performance issues becomes significantly more difficult, potentially leading to extensive downtime and reputational damage. Think of your logs as a detailed record of every interaction with your gateway, providing invaluable insights into its operation and security posture. Analyzing this data allows you to proactively identify and address vulnerabilities before they can be exploited.

A comprehensive logging strategy goes beyond simply recording requests and responses. It involves capturing crucial contextual information, including timestamps, user identities (if applicable), request parameters, response codes, and any errors encountered. This level of detail is essential for forensic analysis in case of a security incident. For instance, tracing a suspicious request back to its origin is much simpler when you have access to comprehensive logs, allowing you to pinpoint the source and quickly neutralize any threats.

Consider the specific types of logs that should be included. Request logs, recording all incoming requests, are fundamental. These logs should include information about the client IP address, request method, URI, headers, and body. Response logs, mirroring information from the responses your gateway sends back, are equally crucial. These should include response codes, headers, and the body size. Error logs are vital for tracking any issues, providing detailed information about the error type, timestamp, and any relevant contextual data. Security logs, detailing authentication attempts, authorization checks, and any security-related events, are essential for identifying and responding to potential breaches.

Implementing effective monitoring is inextricably linked with logging. Real-time monitoring dashboards provide immediate visibility into the health and performance of your API gateway. Monitoring key metrics, like request latency, error rates, and throughput, is essential for proactively identifying and addressing performance bottlenecks. By setting up alerts for critical thresholds, such as excessive error rates or high latency, you can ensure timely intervention, preventing potential service disruptions. Consider integrating your monitoring tools with your logging system to correlate performance metrics with specific events recorded in your logs, facilitating more efficient troubleshooting.

The choice of logging and monitoring tools significantly impacts your ability to effectively manage your API gateway's security. Many solutions offer robust features for centralized log management, real-time monitoring dashboards, and sophisticated alerting capabilities. Evaluate features such as log aggregation, search capabilities, and visualization options. Some services support structured logging, allowing you to easily query and analyze your logs based on specific fields. Ensure the tools you select are scalable to accommodate the expected volume of logs as your API gateway grows, and check that they integrate seamlessly with your existing infrastructure.

Security auditing relies heavily on the quality and availability of your logs. Regularly review your logs to identify suspicious activity, such as unusual request patterns or unauthorized access attempts. Establish a process for analyzing logs, and create alerts to notify you of critical security events. These logs serve as evidence in security investigations, and a robust audit trail can significantly reduce your liability in case of a security breach. Maintaining your logs effectively and safely is as vital as generating them in the first place; ensure secure storage and appropriate access control to safeguard this critical data.

Remember, the effectiveness of your monitoring and logging strategy depends on proactive planning and consistent implementation. Start by defining your logging requirements, considering the specific needs of your application and security policies. Select appropriate tools that align with your requirements, and ensure that your logs are properly indexed and searchable for efficient analysis. Regularly review and refine your monitoring and logging strategy to adapt to evolving threats and operational needs. With a proactive and comprehensive approach, you can leverage monitoring and logging to secure and optimize your API gateway's performance, safeguarding your microservices and ensuring a seamless user experience. Ignoring these crucial aspects will leave your system vulnerable and hinder its long-term success. Make it a priority from the outset. Your future self will thank you.

4 Implementing Authentication Gatekeepers

Integrating with existing identity providers (IdPs) like Okta or Autho streamlines the authentication process significantly. These platforms offer pre-built integrations and robust security features, reducing development time and improving overall security posture. By leveraging their APIs, your API gateway can seamlessly verify user credentials without needing to build and maintain your own authentication infrastructure. This is particularly beneficial for smaller teams or those prioritizing rapid deployment. Consider the specific features offered by each IdP, evaluating factors like ease of integration, cost, and the level of customization they allow. For example, Okta's extensive features might be overkill for a simple application, while Autho's flexibility caters better to complex needs. Remember, selecting the right IdP is a crucial step for a successful implementation. Thoroughly analyze your requirements and choose an IdP that aligns with your project's scope and long-term goals, minimizing unnecessary complexities and maximizing the benefits of a streamlined authentication process.

However, sometimes the standard IdP integrations aren't sufficient. You might need to implement custom authentication flows to meet specific organizational or application requirements. Perhaps you need to integrate with a legacy system, use a non-standard authentication protocol, or implement multi-factor authentication (MFA) with a specific vendor. This often involves creating custom code within the API gateway to handle authentication requests, verify credentials against your internal systems, and generate access tokens. This necessitates a deeper understanding of the API gateway's architecture and programming interfaces. Careful planning and rigorous testing are critical to ensure the security and reliability of any custom solution. Remember to document your custom authentication flows thoroughly, including all steps, security considerations, and error handling mechanisms. This documentation is vital for future maintenance, troubleshooting, and auditing purposes. Always prioritize security best practices in the implementation, incorporating robust input validation and error handling to mitigate potential vulnerabilities.

Building custom authentication flows requires a solid understanding of security principles and best practices. For instance, securely storing and managing secrets, like API keys and database credentials, is paramount. Employing industry-standard encryption techniques and employing secure key management systems are vital to preventing unauthorized access. Moreover, consider using secure coding practices to minimize vulnerabilities in your custom code. Regular security audits and penetration testing help identify and rectify potential weaknesses, while also providing confidence in your implementation's robustness. It's crucial to carefully consider the trade-offs between custom solutions and the benefits of using established IdP integrations. Weigh the development effort, maintainability, and security implications before choosing a custom approach.

When integrating with IdPs or designing custom flows, remember to properly handle authentication failures. Clear and informative error messages guide developers in debugging issues, while robust error handling prevents information leakage that could compromise security. Avoid revealing sensitive internal details in error messages, instead providing generic but helpful information to the client application. Implementing proper logging and monitoring aids in tracking authentication attempts, identifying potential security threats, and providing valuable insights for system improvements. This detailed logging enables post-incident analysis, allowing for improved response times and more effective preventative measures. Comprehensive logging, coupled with real-time monitoring, significantly enhances the security and reliability of the entire authentication system. Effective error handling and logging are crucial for a secure and reliable authentication mechanism. They allow for swift problem resolution, enhancing the overall user experience and protecting sensitive data.

Finally, consider the future scalability of your authentication solution. As your application grows and your user base expands, ensure your authentication system can handle the increased load. Selecting an IdP with robust scalability features or designing your custom flows with scalability in mind is critical. Regular performance testing helps identify bottlenecks and potential scalability issues early on. By proactively addressing scalability challenges, you ensure a smooth and reliable authentication experience for all users, regardless of the application's size or growth rate. This proactive approach minimizes disruptions and maintains user trust and confidence in the application's performance, especially during periods of increased traffic or usage. Continuous monitoring and performance testing are essential to guarantee your authentication system maintains its responsiveness and security under increasing demands.

4.1 Integrating with Identity Providers

Connecting your API gateway to an existing Identity Provider (IdP) significantly streamlines user authentication, eliminating the need to build and maintain your own authentication system. This integration leverages the IdP's existing infrastructure and security expertise, reducing development time and improving overall security posture. Think of it as outsourcing a critical, complex task to a specialist, allowing your team to focus on your core application logic.

Many popular IdPs, such as Okta, Autho, and Azure Active Directory, provide well-documented APIs and SDKs to facilitate this integration. These tools simplify the process of exchanging authentication requests and responses, ensuring seamless user authentication across your microservices. Their robust infrastructure is designed to handle large volumes of authentication requests efficiently and securely. The level of customization offered by these services can significantly influence your workflow.

The integration process typically involves configuring your API gateway to forward authentication requests to the chosen IdP. This often entails setting up appropriate endpoints within your gateway's configuration, specifying the IdP's URL, and configuring the necessary authentication protocols such as OAuth 2.0 or OpenID Connect. You will also need to configure the IdP to recognize your API gateway as a trusted client application, often requiring the generation of client credentials. This is critical for securely authenticating your applications with the IdP.

Once the configuration is complete, user authentication works as follows: a user initiates a request to your API gateway. The gateway redirects the user to the IdP for authentication. Upon successful authentication, the IdP redirects the user back to the gateway with an authentication token, commonly a JSON Web Token (JWT). The gateway verifies this token and grants access to the requested microservice. This process ensures a clear separation of authentication logic from your core API logic, boosting system maintainability.

While the specifics of the integration process vary depending on the chosen IdP and API gateway, the underlying principle remains consistent: securely delegate user authentication to a trusted third party. This reduces the burden on your development team and improves the overall security of your system. However, thorough understanding of the security implications is paramount. You must carefully review the IdP's security certifications, incident response capabilities, and data protection practices. You also have to consider your organization's security policies and compliance requirements. A failure to do so can compromise the whole security posture of your API gateway and potentially lead to data breaches.

Consider the potential need for custom extensions or modifications to accommodate any unique authentication requirements not directly supported by your selected IdP. This might involve custom claim mappings or specific authentication flows tailored to the needs of your application. Well-documented APIs and SDKs often provide extension points for such customizations. Thoroughly investigate these options before you choose an IdP. The implementation might also demand detailed knowledge of security protocols and best practices, such as secure token storage and handling. For example, you might want to integrate with an existing corporate directory, allowing employees to use their corporate credentials for accessing your microservices. This seamless integration significantly enhances user experience, minimizing the need for users to create and manage multiple accounts. Furthermore, it aligns with existing corporate security policies and reduces the management overhead associated with maintaining separate user databases. This approach also allows you to combine different authentication methods based on the user context.

Remember, thorough testing is crucial after integrating with an IdP. Test various authentication scenarios to ensure the seamless operation of the system. Verify proper token handling, response codes, error handling, and access controls. Pay particular attention to scenarios with failed login attempts to ensure the system handles these correctly and is secured against brute force attacks.

In conclusion, integrating with an Identity Provider is a practical and highly effective way to secure your API gateway. It simplifies authentication management, enhances security, and allows your team to focus on application development instead of building and maintaining a complete authentication system. However, it's essential to carefully select an IdP that aligns with your security requirements and to thoroughly test the integration before deployment. This process ensures the security and efficiency of your microservices architecture. Choosing the right IdP is not just about functionality, but also about aligning with your existing security and compliance frameworks.

4.2 Custom Authentication Flows

Sometimes, standard authentication methods like OAuth 2.0 or OpenID Connect aren't sufficient. Your organization might have legacy systems requiring unique authentication protocols, or you might need to integrate with a specialized service that demands a custom approach. This is where crafting custom authentication flows becomes essential. They provide the flexibility to address the unique security and access control needs not readily met by off-the-shelf solutions. Remember, security is a layered approach; a robust, tailored authentication mechanism is a crucial layer in your overall security strategy.

Consider a scenario where you're integrating with an internal system that uses an older, proprietary authentication method. Simply switching to a modern standard might be impractical or impossible due to significant time and resource constraints. A custom flow would allow seamless integration, maintaining access control while avoiding the complexities and costs of a complete system overhaul. The key is to design a solution that aligns with your overall security architecture while also maintaining operational efficiency.

Designing a custom flow begins with a thorough understanding of your specific requirements. Document all aspects of your authentication needs: what systems need access, what level of access is required for each, what authentication methods are currently in place, and what future expansion might necessitate. This detailed analysis enables a systematic design. Failure to fully analyze and document this phase can lead to vulnerabilities and inconsistencies in the overall authentication strategy. Remember, careful planning minimizes future complications.

Once your requirements are clear, you can start designing the custom flow. This involves choosing appropriate technologies and protocols, carefully considering factors like security, performance, and maintainability. For example, you might use a combination of certificates, API keys, and perhaps even a custom-built token generation and validation service to tailor the authentication process precisely to your needs. Remember, security should always be paramount in this design process.

Implementing a custom flow within your API gateway requires careful integration. You'll need to configure the gateway to recognize and process the custom authentication headers or parameters. This often involves writing custom code or scripts to interact with the authentication system. This part requires expertise in the specific API gateway technology and programming languages. Thorough testing is crucial before deployment to identify any flaws or vulnerabilities. Rigorous testing helps ensure a secure and reliable authentication process.

Maintaining your custom authentication flow is as crucial as its implementation. Regular security audits, updates to address new vulnerabilities, and ongoing monitoring are essential. Security is an ongoing process, not a one-time task. Regular reviews of your security protocols and procedures are vital to ensure your systems remain protected. These steps will help prevent breaches and maintain a high level of security.

Finally, remember that scalability is a key consideration. Your custom flow must be able to handle a growing number of requests and users without compromising performance or security. Carefully plan for growth to avoid future bottlenecks or vulnerabilities. Scaling your authentication system is critical for supporting the growth of your applications and services.

Creating custom authentication flows for your API gateway allows for fine-grained control and integration with legacy or specialized systems. However, the complexity requires careful planning, secure implementation, and diligent maintenance. By understanding your specific requirements, employing robust security practices, and proactively addressing potential challenges, you can effectively leverage custom authentication flows to bolster your overall microservices security posture. The benefits of this approach – enhanced security and greater control – make the effort worthwhile, even with its additional complexity. Ultimately, a well-designed custom flow provides the tailored security your organization needs. The key to success lies in meticulous design, robust implementation, and a commitment to ongoing maintenance and improvement.

5 Microservices Architecture and API Gateways

Microservices, with their independent deployments and specialized functionalities, present unique security challenges. A well-structured microservices architecture, however, leverages API gateways to effectively manage these challenges. Think of it as a single point of entry, a security fortress protecting your individual services from direct external access. This centralized approach simplifies security management, allowing you to implement consistent security policies across your entire system. Implementing robust authentication and authorization at the gateway level significantly reduces the attack surface of each individual microservice.

Designing secure microservices means prioritizing security from the ground up. Each service should be built with minimal attack surface in mind. This involves using secure coding practices, regularly updating dependencies, and thoroughly testing for vulnerabilities. Employing least privilege access control principles and adhering to secure design patterns are crucial components in this defensive posture. Avoid exposing sensitive data unnecessarily; always encrypt data in transit and at rest. Remember, securing each individual component significantly improves the overall security of the entire system.

API gateway deployment strategies significantly impact both security and scalability. A single gateway can handle a large volume of requests, but distributing the load across multiple gateways enhances resilience and fault tolerance. Consider using a geographically distributed architecture to reduce latency and improve availability. Choosing the right deployment strategy, whether it's on-premises, cloud-based, or a hybrid approach, significantly impacts your operational efficiency and security posture. This careful consideration is a critical element of maintaining a robust microservices ecosystem.

Observability and monitoring are paramount for maintaining a secure and reliable microservices architecture. Real-time monitoring allows for the immediate detection of security breaches and performance bottlenecks. This includes implementing comprehensive logging, tracing, and metrics collection. Using these insights, you can identify anomalies, investigate security incidents promptly, and proactively address potential vulnerabilities. Effective monitoring isn't just about reacting to problems; it's about preventing them from occurring in the first place. This proactive approach is key to building a resilient and secure system. Investing in the right monitoring tools and establishing comprehensive alerts is crucial for ensuring your system's security and preventing disruptions.

Centralized logging is also critical. An API gateway acts as a central point for all API requests, meaning a single location for log aggregation provides a comprehensive overview of all activity across all services. This centralized approach simplifies security auditing and incident response. Effective log analysis can reveal patterns of malicious activity and assist in pinpointing the source of security breaches. A robust logging and monitoring system is a cornerstone of a secure microservices architecture. Properly implementing these features will allow you to identify and mitigate threats proactively

and quickly.
Consider the advantages of employing various security mechanisms within the gateway. These include input validation, rate limiting, and the implementation of security headers such as HSTS (HTTP Strict Transport Security) and CSP (Content Security Policy). These mechanisms prevent common attacks such as cross-site scripting (XSS) and SQL injection, while also enhancing performance and overall stability. These proactive defenses can substantially strengthen your API's security posture.
Remember, security is an ongoing process, not a one-time activity. Regular security assessments, penetration testing, and vulnerability scanning are crucial for maintaining the security of your microservices architecture. Proactively addressing vulnerabilities and improving your security posture is crucial for maintaining the integrity and confidentiality of your data. Staying up-to-date on the latest security threats and best practices is essential in today's ever-evolving threat landscape. Regular updates, security patches, and rigorous testing are essential elements in ensuring long-term security.
Finally, integrating your API gateway with existing identity providers can simplify user authentication. Platforms like Okta or Autho offer robust authentication and authorization capabilities that can be readily integrated into your API gateway, reducing the need for building custom authentication flows. This integration streamlines development and improves overall security by leveraging established and well-tested identity management systems. Such integrations provide a smoother user experience and a more streamlined security process. Therefore, implementing proper authentication processes throughout your API gateway workflow is essential to secure user data and maintain a robust and reliable system.

5.1 Designing Secure Microservices

Secure microservices demand a meticulous approach; their decentralized nature necessitates robust security measures at every level. Ignoring this critical aspect can lead to vulnerabilities that compromise the entire system, causing significant financial and reputational damage. We must consider security not as an afterthought, but as an integral part of the design process, from the initial conception to deployment and beyond.

A fundamental principle is the principle of least privilege. Each microservice should only possess the minimal permissions required for its specific function. Overly permissive access rights create attack vectors, greatly increasing the potential impact of successful breaches. Implementing role-based access control (RBAC) effectively manages these permissions, ensuring that each microservice only accesses the resources absolutely necessary for its operation. This granular control significantly reduces the risk of lateral movement within the system, should one microservice be compromised.

Communication between microservices should be encrypted using secure protocols like HTTPS. This ensures data confidentiality and integrity, preventing eavesdropping and data manipulation. Furthermore, consider employing mutual TLS (mTLS) authentication, where each microservice authenticates itself to others using digital certificates. This adds an extra layer of security, authenticating not only the user but also the microservice initiating the request. This approach reduces the risk of unauthorized access even if an attacker gains access to a network segment.

Input validation and sanitization are crucial aspects of secure microservice design. Never trust user input; always thoroughly validate and sanitize it before processing. This prevents common vulnerabilities like SQL injection, cross-site scripting (XSS), and command injection. This seemingly simple step significantly reduces the attack surface and prevents many serious security flaws, bolstering the security of your microservices significantly. Regular security audits and penetration testing should be incorporated into your development lifecycle. This proactive approach identifies vulnerabilities before they can be exploited by malicious actors.

Leveraging a robust API gateway provides a central point for security policy enforcement, acting as a crucial intermediary between clients and your microservices. The API gateway can implement rate limiting, input validation, and authentication mechanisms, providing a consolidated security posture. This centralized approach simplifies security management and enhances overall system security. Integrating a comprehensive monitoring and logging system is also critical. This provides insights into microservice behavior, enabling rapid detection of anomalous activity that may indicate an attack.

Remember, security is not a one-time task but an ongoing process. Regular security assessments, code reviews, and penetration testing help identify and mitigate vulnerabilities before they can be exploited. Stay up-to-date with the latest security threats and vulnerabilities; proactively implement patches and updates. Remember that the responsibility for security isn't solely on the development team. Collaboration and communication are essential across all teams involved in the system's lifecycle; involving operations and security teams from the start is paramount.

Furthermore, consider implementing circuit breakers to prevent cascading failures. If one microservice becomes unavailable, the circuit breaker prevents repeated requests that would further strain the system. This approach helps maintain system stability even under duress, mitigating the impact of failures and attacks. Regularly review your security policies and update them as needed, particularly as your system grows and evolves.

Properly designed and implemented, microservices can offer significant advantages in terms of scalability, maintainability, and resilience. However, without a strong security foundation, these advantages are negated by the increased attack surface. Prioritizing security from the outset ensures that your microservices remain secure, reliable, and able to withstand modern cyber threats. A proactive, integrated, and iterative security approach is paramount in creating a resilient and secure system. The importance of keeping your microservices up-to-date with the latest security patches and configurations should never be underestimated. Neglecting this aspect can leave your system vulnerable to easily preventable attacks. Treat security as an ongoing conversation, not a one-time fix. Continuous improvement and adaptation are essential in the ever-evolving landscape of cybersecurity. This consistent focus on security ensures the long-term health and integrity of your microservices architecture.

5.2 API Gateway Deployment Strategies

Successful API gateway deployment hinges on careful planning and execution. Choosing the right deployment strategy directly impacts your microservices' security, scalability, and overall performance. A poorly planned deployment can lead to bottlenecks, security vulnerabilities, and operational nightmares, ultimately undermining the very benefits an API gateway promises. Therefore, understanding your options is crucial before you start. Consider your infrastructure. Are you using a cloud provider like AWS, Azure, or Google Cloud? Each offers managed API gateway services, simplifying deployment and maintenance. These services usually handle infrastructure management, scaling, and security updates, letting you focus on your APIs. However, a vendor lock-in is a potential disadvantage; switching providers later could be complex.

On-premises deployment offers more control but requires more effort. You'll manage the servers, software updates, security patching, and scaling yourself. This approach works best for organizations with specific security requirements or existing on-premises infrastructure they want to leverage. The increased operational overhead, though, must be carefully weighed against the potential benefits of enhanced control and customization.

Hybrid deployments combine the benefits of both cloud and on-premises approaches. Some APIs might reside on-premises due to regulatory compliance or legacy system integration, while others, especially newer ones, could benefit from the scalability and elasticity of the cloud. This flexibility allows for a tailored solution, optimizing for both cost and performance, but adds complexity in management and coordination between different environments.

Deployment patterns matter too. A single API gateway instance might suffice for smaller deployments, but as your system scales, you'll likely need a multi-instance setup for increased availability and resilience. Consider load balancing to distribute traffic effectively, preventing overload on any single instance. Employing techniques such as active-passive or active-active configurations helps mitigate potential downtime. Active-passive pairs one active gateway with a standby; the standby automatically takes over if the primary fails. Active-active distributes traffic among multiple gateways, increasing capacity and fault tolerance.

Furthermore, carefully consider your scaling strategy. Will you scale vertically (increasing resources of existing instances) or horizontally (adding more instances)? Horizontal scaling, generally, offers better scalability and resilience compared to vertical scaling, which is limited by the hardware capabilities of your servers. However, horizontal scaling involves more complex management of multiple instances and the coordinating software needed to keep things working seamlessly.

Remember the importance of monitoring and logging. Regardless of the chosen deployment strategy, robust monitoring is essential. Tracking key metrics such as latency, error rates, and request volumes helps you identify bottlenecks and potential issues. Comprehensive logging provides crucial information for debugging, security auditing, and capacity planning. Integrating your API gateway with your existing monitoring and logging infrastructure is critical for effective system management.

Finally, security is paramount. In addition to using secure protocols like HTTPS and implementing appropriate security headers, consider using network segmentation and access controls to restrict access to your API gateway and underlying infrastructure. Regular security audits and penetration testing should be part of your ongoing operations to proactively identify and address potential vulnerabilities. A well-secured API gateway is the cornerstone of a robust and trustworthy microservices architecture. Neglecting security can create significant vulnerabilities and risks, potentially leading to data breaches or system disruptions. Prioritize security measures from the very beginning of your deployment strategy. The long-term cost of a security breach far outweighs the upfront investment in securing your gateway.

5.3 Observability and Monitoring

Effective monitoring and observability are crucial for maintaining the security and reliability of your API gateway and the microservices it protects. Without them, identifying and resolving issues becomes a significant challenge, potentially leading to security breaches or performance degradation. Think of it like this: you wouldn't drive a car without checking the dashboard, would you? Similarly, you shouldn't manage a complex system like an API gateway without constant monitoring.

Implementing robust observability requires a multi-faceted approach. Start by strategically instrumenting your gateway and microservices. This involves integrating logging, metrics, and tracing capabilities into every component. Comprehensive logging provides detailed records of all API requests, responses, and errors. Detailed logs are essential for tracking security incidents, debugging performance issues, and performing security audits. Choose a logging system capable of handling high volumes of data efficiently, like Elasticsearch with Logstash and Kibana (ELK stack), or a cloud-based logging service. Crucially, ensure your logs are structured for easier analysis and searching, enabling rapid identification of relevant information.

Beyond simple logging, incorporate metrics to gather quantitative data on various aspects of your system's performance and health. Think response times, request rates, error rates, and resource utilization. These metrics should be collected in real-time and aggregated to provide a comprehensive overview of your gateway's operational status. Tools like Prometheus and Grafana offer powerful visualizations and alerting capabilities, helping you identify and respond to anomalies promptly. Configure alerts for critical metrics to receive immediate notification of any potentially disruptive events.

Distributed tracing becomes especially vital in microservices architecture. Requests often traverse multiple services, making it challenging to pinpoint the source of errors or performance bottlenecks. Distributed tracing allows you to follow a single request through its entire journey, from the API gateway to the backend microservices and back. Tools like Jaeger and Zipkin offer excellent support for distributed tracing, helping you visualize the flow of requests and identify any performance bottlenecks or points of failure within individual microservices. By meticulously tracking the path of each request, you gain a deeper understanding of the underlying system's behavior.

Properly configured alerts are essential for effective monitoring. Don't just rely on manual checks. Set up automated alerts based on pre-defined thresholds for key metrics, such as high error rates, prolonged response times, or significant spikes in request volume. These alerts should be routed to appropriate teams or individuals responsible for handling incidents. Implement a well-defined incident management process to ensure prompt and efficient response to alerts. This process should include clear escalation paths, communication channels, and runbooks detailing steps to resolve specific issues. Consider using dedicated incident management tools to streamline the process and enhance collaboration among teams.

Observability is not merely about reacting to issues; it's also about proactively identifying potential problems. Regularly review your monitoring data to identify trends and patterns. Look for gradual performance degradations or unusual spikes in error rates that might indicate underlying issues. Use this information to proactively address potential problems before they escalate into major incidents. Proactive maintenance based on observed trends is far more effective than reacting to crises. This allows for a more predictable and stable system.

Finally, remember that choosing the right tools and implementing them effectively is only half the battle. Training your team on how to use and interpret monitoring data is just as critical. Ensure your team is well-versed in the tools used, can effectively analyze the data generated, and understands how to respond to different types of alerts. This ensures efficient problem resolution and minimizes downtime. Regular training and knowledge sharing will create a more informed and efficient team. Without a skilled team capable of interpreting and acting on the data collected, even the most sophisticated monitoring system will fail to achieve its objectives.

6 Advanced API Gateway Features

Efficient API versioning is crucial for maintaining backward compatibility while introducing new features. Employ a clear versioning strategy, such as semantic versioning (major.minor.patch), to indicate breaking changes and allow clients to seamlessly transition to updated versions. This prevents disruptions and allows for iterative development without sacrificing stability. Properly managing different API versions requires robust tooling within your API gateway; consider features that automate the deprecation process, notifying clients of upcoming changes and providing ample time for migration. This minimizes downtime and disruption during updates. Furthermore, a well-structured versioning system allows for easier maintenance and updates, improving the overall lifecycle of your APIs and reducing the technical debt. Failing to implement proper versioning can result in compatibility issues, increased maintenance overhead, and ultimately, dissatisfied clients. Therefore, a well-planned API versioning strategy is essential for long-term API success.

Caching strategies significantly impact API performance and responsiveness. Implement caching mechanisms within your API gateway to reduce the load on backend services and improve response times. Employ different caching levels, such as edge caching for static content and server-side caching for frequently accessed data. Careful consideration must be given to caching policies, including cache invalidation strategies to maintain data consistency. For example, implementing a cache invalidation strategy based on time-to-live (TTL) or using a cache invalidation mechanism linked to data changes is critical. Remember, overly aggressive caching can lead to stale data, so finding the right balance between performance gains and data freshness is essential. Optimizing caching requires monitoring performance metrics to identify areas for improvement and fine-tuning caching parameters. By thoughtfully implementing and managing caching, you can significantly enhance your API's overall performance and user experience.

Advanced traffic management capabilities within your API gateway are paramount for ensuring high availability and resilience. Implement features such as load balancing to distribute traffic across multiple backend instances, preventing overload and maximizing uptime. This ensures that your application remains responsive even under heavy loads, preventing failures and ensuring a positive user experience. Furthermore, consider implementing circuit breakers and rate limiting to mitigate the impact of failures and prevent abuse. Circuit breakers automatically stop routing traffic to failing services, preventing cascading failures, and rate limiting controls the rate of incoming requests, preventing denial-of-service attacks. Implementing these features improves the system's resilience against failures and attacks, safeguarding the API's availability. Active monitoring and dynamic adjustments of traffic routing based on real-time performance metrics are also crucial for maximizing the effectiveness of your traffic management strategy. Proactive monitoring will alert you of potential problems in real-time, providing ample time for intervention before a failure impacts the API's availability. A robust traffic management system is vital for providing a reliable and scalable API experience.

6.1 API Versioning and Management

Effective API versioning is crucial for maintaining backward compatibility while introducing new features and improvements. Ignoring this aspect can lead to fractured applications and frustrated developers relying on your API. You need a clear strategy, and that begins with choosing a suitable versioning scheme. URI versioning, where the version is included in the API endpoint's URL (e.g., /v1/users), is straightforward and widely understood. However, it can become cumbersome with many versions, cluttering your URL structure. Header-based versioning, using a custom HTTP header (like X-API-Version), offers a cleaner approach, keeping URLs concise. It's more flexible; however, it requires careful client-side handling to ensure correct versioning. Finally, content negotiation, using the Accept header, offers a more sophisticated approach, letting clients specify the desired version through the media type (e.g., application/vnd.yourcompany.v1+json). It provides flexibility, but necessitates robust server-side handling of media type negotiation. The selection depends on your specific needs and architectural preferences; considering your scaling strategy early prevents future headaches.

Implementing your chosen scheme requires careful planning and execution. Documentation is paramount; clearly outlining the available API versions, their functionalities, and any deprecation policies keeps everyone informed. Thorough testing across different versions is equally important to ensure smooth transitions and prevent regressions. Consider using a versioning management tool, allowing for automation and centralized control over your API versions. These tools can manage the lifecycle of different versions, from release to deprecation, minimizing manual intervention and streamlining your workflow. Proper logging and monitoring provide insights into usage patterns and identify potential problems before they escalate. Observing API usage allows for better decision-making regarding deprecation schedules and resource allocation. This data-driven approach ensures your API remains efficient and aligned with evolving user requirements.

Deprecation of older API versions is an inevitable part of API evolution. However, a poorly managed deprecation process can severely impact your users. Establish a clear communication strategy, providing ample notice before sunsetting an older version. This is crucial for developers to adapt and update their applications without disruptions. Offer sufficient transition time, enabling developers to move seamlessly between versions, and provide comprehensive documentation on the updates, new endpoints, and any changes in the data structures. Consider maintaining minimal support for deprecated versions, offering them for a specific period to allow for a smoother migration. This is a balance between progress and user experience, avoiding abrupt changes that break existing applications. Gradual deprecation provides a smooth migration and reduces the risk of significant service disruptions.

Beyond choosing a versioning scheme, designing your API for version compatibility is critical. Adopt a strategy that minimizes breaking changes. For instance, avoid renaming or removing existing endpoints without providing clear alternatives. Preserve existing data structures, introducing new fields instead of altering existing ones whenever possible. Design your API using features like conditional request handling, allowing for different responses based on the API version requested, facilitating compatibility across multiple versions. A well-structured API minimizes the impact of new versions on existing clients. Furthermore, consider using forward-compatibility strate-

gies which allow clients designed for an older version to still interact with newer versions of your API without any issues. A comprehensive approach considers both backward and forward compatibility.
Managing multiple API versions efficiently requires a robust infrastructure. Consider implementing a dedicated API gateway to handle routing and version negotiation. This centralizes management and simplifies the process of directing requests to the correct version of your API. Automating tasks like version deployment and monitoring through CI/CD pipelines ensures smooth, error-free updates and provides insights into the performance of different versions. Adopting a mature development process, with rigorous testing and code review, reduces the likelihood of introducing bugs and inconsistencies across API versions. This structured approach reduces maintenance burdens and ensures the overall health of your API ecosystem. Remember, diligent version management is a core component of building a sustainable and reliable API; it is an ongoing process, demanding consistent effort and proactive adaptation. Proactive planning, consistent communication, and robust infrastructure contribute to a smooth and efficient API management strategy.

6.2 Caching and Performance Optimization

Caching strategically within your API gateway is paramount for performance. Imagine a scenario: thousands of identical requests flood your system, each demanding the same data. Without caching, your backend microservices laboriously process each request, resulting in slow response times and potentially overwhelming your infrastructure. Caching intercepts these repetitive requests, serving pre-fetched responses from a fast, readily accessible store. This dramatically reduces the load on your backend, resulting in significantly faster response times for users. Think of it as a high-speed memory for frequently accessed information.

The selection of the right caching strategy is critical. Consider the nature of your data. Is it static, meaning it rarely changes (like a product catalog)? Or dynamic, frequently updated (like real-time stock prices)? Static data benefits from long-lived caches, holding the data for extended periods. For dynamic data, you'll likely use short-lived caches, updated frequently to reflect changes. Proper caching strategy isn't a one-size-fits-all solution; it requires careful consideration of data characteristics.

Choosing the appropriate cache technology is equally important. Popular options include Redis, Memcached, and even in-memory caches provided by your API gateway itself. Redis, known for its flexibility and persistence, excels for complex caching needs. Memcached, prioritizing speed, is ideal for simple key-value caching. Your API gateway's built-in cache may be sufficient for less demanding applications, offering a convenient and streamlined solution. Thoroughly evaluate your specific requirements—data volume, access patterns, and performance goals—to make an informed decision.

Effective cache invalidation is crucial. Stale data served from the cache can be worse than no data at all. Implementing a robust invalidation strategy ensures your cache always reflects the current state of your backend. Techniques range from time-based expiration (setting a time limit for cached data) to cache-aside patterns (checking for data updates before serving cached content). Even advanced strategies like using publish-subscribe mechanisms for real-time updates can be employed. Remember, a poorly invalidated cache can lead to inconsistencies and errors.

Beyond simple caching, consider advanced techniques like caching at multiple levels. This layered approach involves caching responses at various points in your API gateway pipeline and even within your microservices. You could cache responses at the gateway level for frequently accessed data, then further refine this by caching specific data points within individual microservices. Such a multi-tiered setup dramatically enhances overall performance by distributing the caching load and reducing latency.

Monitoring your cache performance is essential. Track metrics like cache hit rate (the percentage of requests served from the cache), eviction rate (the frequency of removing data from the cache), and cache latency (time taken to retrieve data from the cache). A high hit rate signifies efficient caching. Low latency demonstrates fast access. These metrics provide invaluable insights into the health and effectiveness of your caching strategy, guiding optimizations and improvements. Regularly reviewing these analytics is key for maintaining optimal performance.

Integrating your caching strategy with your gateway's security measures is critical. Ensure your caching mechanism does not inadvertently expose sensitive data. For example, avoid caching responses containing personally identifiable information (PII) unless strictly necessary and with adequate protection. Security considerations should always be paramount. A well-designed cache enhances performance without compromising security.

Finally, remember that caching is not a silver bullet. While it offers significant performance benefits, it's not a solution for every performance issue. It's vital to identify performance bottlenecks systematically and address them using various techniques, with caching as one valuable tool in your arsenal. Profiling your applications, identifying slow database queries, or optimizing network communications might prove equally, if not more, impactful in certain cases. A balanced approach is essential for achieving optimal performance. Over-reliance on caching alone can mask other underlying issues that need to be resolved.

6.3 Traffic Management and Routing

Efficient traffic management is paramount for any API gateway, ensuring optimal performance and high availability. Without robust routing strategies, your microservices might struggle under heavy loads, leading to slow response times or even complete outages. Imagine a scenario with a surge in requests – without proper management, some services become overwhelmed while others sit idle. This chapter provides the solutions you need to prevent that.

Consider load balancing as your first line of defense. Distributing traffic across multiple instances of a microservice prevents any single instance from becoming a bottleneck. Round-robin, least-connections, and weighted round-robin are common algorithms. Choosing the right algorithm depends on your specific needs and the characteristics of your microservices. For instance, a weighted round-robin might be preferred if some microservices handle more computationally intensive tasks and require more resources. Implementing these algorithms is relatively straightforward and can drastically improve overall performance.

Moving beyond simple load balancing, you can implement sophisticated routing rules based on various criteria. Headers, query parameters, and even the client's IP address can be used to direct traffic to the appropriate microservice version or instance. This level of control is vital for supporting different API versions, managing canary deployments, or directing specific users to dedicated environments. Imagine A/B testing a new feature, using header-based routing to direct a subset of users to the updated version while the majority remains on the stable one, allowing for a gradual rollout and minimizing disruption.

Furthermore, advanced features like traffic mirroring and shadowing provide invaluable support during deployments or testing. Traffic mirroring copies a percentage of the incoming traffic to a shadow instance of your microservice, allowing you to test and validate updates in a real-world environment without impacting production users directly. Shadowing, similar to mirroring, but allows for testing interactions without exposing the shadow instance to the main flow. This is an extremely useful strategy to reduce risks and validate changes in a controlled manner. These capabilities reduce risk, improve confidence in deployments, and simplify the continuous integration and continuous delivery (CI/CD) pipelines.

Another crucial aspect is the implementation of circuit breakers. These prevent cascading failures by stopping requests to a failing microservice, thus protecting other components of your system. When a microservice experiences prolonged unavailability or errors, the circuit breaker automatically prevents further calls, thereby preventing propagation of failure throughout your system. This strategy, coupled with appropriate retry logic, ensures resilience and prevents a single point of failure from bringing down your entire infrastructure. You can define thresholds for opening and closing the circuit breaker based on failure rate or latency, and configure the retry mechanisms to suit your application requirements.

Fault tolerance is another critical consideration. Your gateway must gracefully handle failures and ensure continuous operation even when one or more of your microservices are down. Techniques like retries and fallback mechanisms are essential components. Retries allow the system to automatically attempt failed requests again after a short delay, while fallback mechanisms provide alternative responses when a primary service is unreachable. A robust strategy would employ both in tandem; retries give the primary service another opportunity to fulfill the request, while the fallback safeguards against protracted unavailability. This ensures a smooth user experience, even in the face of temporary outages. The exact implementation of retries and fallbacks depends on your microservice architecture and operational requirements.

Finally, comprehensive monitoring and logging are indispensable. Real-time monitoring provides insights into traffic patterns, response times, and error rates, alerting you to potential problems before they impact your users. Logging is crucial for post-incident analysis, helping you identify the root cause of outages and refine your traffic management strategies. A combination of metrics and logs allows for deep analysis, pinpointing areas for improvement and informing proactive measures to enhance overall system stability. It's essential to establish a detailed logging policy that captures meaningful data, with a plan to analyze and act on the logs to continuously improve system reliability. Combining this with alerting, creates a robust self-healing system. Proper implementation allows for automated responses to events that demand immediate attention, enabling quicker recovery from disruptive events.

7 Case Studies and Future Trends

Netflix, a streaming giant, relies heavily on API gateways to manage the massive traffic to its microservices. Their implementation demonstrates the scalability and resilience needed to handle millions of concurrent users, showcasing the power of a well-architected gateway in distributing load across multiple servers and ensuring high availability. This case study highlights not only the importance of proper gateway configuration but also the sophisticated monitoring and logging systems necessary to identify and react to potential issues before they impact the user experience. The sheer volume of data processed daily underscores the need for efficient caching mechanisms to minimize latency and improve the overall performance of their platform. Their success story emphasizes the crucial role of a robust, well-maintained API gateway in supporting a high-traffic, globally distributed application. Furthermore, their detailed logging and monitoring capabilities facilitate proactive security maintenance, identifying potential vulnerabilities and addressing them before exploitation. Their continuous investment in upgrading their gateway infrastructure highlights the ever-evolving nature of API security and the need for constant adaptation to new threats and technological advancements. The ability to seamlessly handle unexpected surges in demand speaks volumes about the importance of scalability in the design and implementation of an effective API gateway, making them a benchmark for industry best practices.

The rise of serverless architectures presents exciting opportunities for API gateway development. Integrating serverless functions with API gateways offers a more efficient and cost-effective way to handle specific tasks, such as authentication or authorization, without requiring the maintenance of dedicated servers. This shift towards serverless reduces operational overhead and increases scalability, allowing developers to focus on core application logic rather than infrastructure management. The flexibility of serverless functions also enhances the extensibility of API gateways, enabling the seamless incorporation of new functionalities and integrations as needed. This approach allows for dynamic scaling based on real-time demands, resulting in improved cost optimization and resource utilization. Furthermore, serverless functions provide a natural platform for implementing advanced security measures, such as fine-grained access control and real-time threat detection, improving the overall security posture of the system. The integration of AI-powered threat detection systems within serverless function-based API gateways represents a significant advancement in the field. This development significantly enhances security capabilities by automatically identifying and mitigating potential threats in real time, significantly reducing the response time for security incidents.

While API gateways provide significant security advantages, they also introduce new attack vectors. For example, attackers might attempt to exploit vulnerabilities within the gateway itself, bypassing security measures designed for individual microservices. This necessitates a multi-layered security approach, encompassing secure coding practices for the gateway itself, along with regular security audits and penetration testing. Moreover, robust monitoring and logging mechanisms are crucial to detect and respond to potential attacks promptly. This includes analyzing traffic patterns for anomalies and implementing intrusion detection systems to identify malicious activity. A comprehensive security strategy needs to consider both the gateway and the individual microservices it protects, ensuring a holistic approach to security management. Advanced encryption techniques and data loss prevention (DLP) solutions, often integrated at the gateway level, further fortify the security architecture. The ongoing evolution of threat landscapes necessitates a proactive and adaptive approach to API gateway security, demanding continuous updates and improvements to counter emerging threats and vulnerabilities.

Looking ahead, we can anticipate several key trends in API security. The growing adoption of GraphQL, with its efficient data fetching capabilities, poses unique security challenges that require specific mitigation strategies, particularly regarding authorization and data filtering. Similarly, the integration of WebAssembly (Wasm) into API gateways holds promise for improving performance and security, enabling the execution of security-sensitive code in a sandboxed environment, but introduces complexity in management and security considerations. Furthermore, the increasing use of decentralized identity systems, such as those based on blockchain technology, will transform how we authenticate and authorize API access. These changes will require a shift in how we approach API security, demanding new tools and techniques to ensure the integrity and confidentiality of data exchanged via APIs. Further research in decentralized and cryptographic identity management systems will play a crucial role in developing robust and future-proof API security solutions. The ongoing advancements in AI and machine learning also hold the potential to enhance API security significantly, providing advanced threat detection and mitigation capabilities.

These are not mere speculations, but emerging technologies that are reshaping the entire API security landscape.
In conclusion, the effective deployment of API gateways is critical for securing microservices architectures in modern applications. Understanding real-world examples, considering emerging technologies, and proactively addressing potential threats are essential for building robust and secure systems. The future of API security will be characterized by continuous innovation, demanding ongoing learning and adaptation to stay ahead of the curve. This ongoing need for adaptation underscores the importance of both proactive and reactive security measures, ensuring that the security strategy is both robust and responsive to the ever-evolving threat landscape. The combination of comprehensive security practices, coupled with a proactive approach to new technologies and threats, is the cornerstone of building a secure and reliable system in the ever-changing world of API security. Constant vigilance and adaptation are essential elements to ensure long-term success.

7.1 Real-World API Gateway Implementations

Kong, a popular open-source API gateway, offers a robust solution for managing microservices. Its plugin architecture allows for easy customization and extension, adding functionalities like authentication, rate limiting, and logging without complex coding. Consider a scenario where a financial institution uses Kong to secure its mobile banking application. The API gateway acts as the single entry point for all mobile requests, enforcing stringent security policies such as multi-factor authentication and rate limiting to prevent fraud. Kong's plugin system enables seamless integration with existing security infrastructure and allows for granular control over access permissions based on user roles and device characteristics. The flexibility offered by Kong allows for adapting to evolving security threats and business requirements, making it a powerful tool for securing mission-critical applications. This adaptability is crucial for applications dealing with sensitive user data, ensuring a resilient and secure system.

Let's examine another example: a large e-commerce platform using Apigee, a cloud-based API gateway. Apigee offers advanced features like traffic management and analytics, which are invaluable for a high-traffic application. For example, the e-commerce platform could use Apigee to route traffic intelligently, directing peak loads to multiple servers to prevent performance degradation. Apigee's built-in analytics provides insights into API usage, which helps identify potential bottlenecks and optimize performance. This granular control, coupled with comprehensive analytics, enables the e-commerce company to improve both the user experience and operational efficiency. Moreover, Apigee offers advanced security features, ensuring secure transactions and protecting sensitive customer data. The combination of traffic management, analytics and security makes Apigee particularly well-suited for large-scale e-commerce platforms dealing with significant traffic volumes and sensitive data.

Consider the implementation challenges. Migrating existing applications to use an API gateway often requires significant planning and coordination. Careful consideration must be given to factors such as existing infrastructure, security policies, and development processes. For example, integrating the API gateway with existing authentication systems and security tools might require custom development or configuration. This may lead to potential delays and increased costs. Thorough testing is essential to ensure the gateway functions correctly and integrates seamlessly with existing systems.

This includes conducting both unit and integration tests to identify and address potential issues before deployment. A well-defined migration strategy, thorough planning, and rigorous testing are key to ensuring a smooth and successful transition.

A crucial aspect of API gateway implementation is monitoring and logging. Real-time monitoring allows you to quickly identify and address issues affecting the performance and security of your APIs. Comprehensive logging provides valuable insights for auditing purposes and for troubleshooting any problems. Imagine a situation where a denial-of-service attack targets your API gateway. Effective monitoring would instantly alert you to the attack, allowing you to implement mitigation strategies. Moreover, detailed logging would help identify the source and nature of the attack, enabling you to improve your security posture and prevent future attacks. Comprehensive monitoring and robust logging are vital components of a secure and resilient API gateway architecture.

Choosing the right API gateway is vital; factors like scalability, security features, ease of integration, and cost must be weighed. Open-source gateways offer flexibility and cost-effectiveness, while commercial options provide additional features and support. However, selecting the appropriate gateway heavily depends on the specific needs and requirements of your application and infrastructure. A small startup with limited resources might opt for an open-source solution, while a large enterprise might prioritize a commercial solution with advanced features and support. The decision-making process involves a comprehensive evaluation, considering cost, scalability, security, support, and integration with existing systems.

Finally, remember that API gateway implementation is not a one-time event. Regular security updates, performance optimization, and feature enhancements are necessary to ensure continued security and performance.

Continuous monitoring and adaptation to evolving security threats and technological advancements are essential for maintaining a robust and reliable API gateway infrastructure. Ignoring these aspects can leave your system vulnerable to attacks and compromise the security and performance of your applications. A proactive approach to maintenance and updates is crucial for maintaining a secure and effective API gateway system.

7.2 Emerging Technologies and Trends

The landscape of API security is constantly evolving, driven by the relentless innovation in technology. Serverless architectures, for instance, are gaining significant traction, presenting both opportunities and challenges for API gateway implementation. Their inherent scalability and cost-effectiveness are compelling, but integrating them seamlessly with existing security infrastructures requires careful planning and the adoption of new strategies for authentication and authorization. This necessitates a shift towards more dynamic and context-aware security policies, capable of adapting to the ephemeral nature of serverless functions. Consider the complexities of managing access control across multiple ephemeral compute instances, a far cry from traditional, static server deployments. Successful integration demands deep understanding and careful selection of serverless-compatible API gateways and authentication tools.

Moving beyond serverless, the growing adoption of GraphQL APIs introduces a unique set of security considerations. Unlike RESTful APIs, GraphQL's query language allows clients to request specific data fields, potentially exposing sensitive information through insufficiently controlled queries. This demands a granular approach to authorization, going beyond simple role-based access control and implementing field-level permissions.

This is a significant shift in the traditional approach to authorization, needing intricate design and robust implementation. Consider that building this kind of authorization system for GraphQL requires specialized tools and a meticulous understanding of data modeling and security principles. Failure to implement these granular controls can lead to serious data breaches.

Another significant trend is the rise of WebAssembly (Wasm). This technology allows developers to compile code written in languages like C++ or Rust into a portable binary format that runs in a sandboxed environment within a web browser or server. Wasm is poised to revolutionize how we handle computationally intensive tasks within API gateways, enabling more sophisticated security features and performance optimizations. However, the security implications of Wasm are still under active research. Securely managing Wasm modules within the gateway, ensuring that they do not compromise system integrity, is vital. This requires rigorous validation and monitoring of all Wasm code. Moreover, effective deployment strategies and robust sandboxing mechanisms are required, demanding a new level of vigilance.

The increasing reliance on machine learning (ML) for various aspects of API security is yet another critical factor. ML algorithms are being deployed to detect anomalies and malicious activities in real-time, providing more proactive protection against advanced attacks. However, integrating ML models requires careful consideration of data bias and model robustness. A flawed ML model might lead to false positives or, even worse, fail to identify genuine attacks, jeopardizing the entire system. The complexity of model training, deployment, and ongoing monitoring necessitates a dedicated team and rigorous testing. Ensuring the security and reliability of these ML models are critical to their success.

Finally, the quantum computing threat looms large. While still in its nascent stages, the potential impact of quantum computing on current cryptographic algorithms cannot be ignored. It is essential that API security strategies begin to consider the future requirements for post-quantum cryptography. This involves evaluating and implementing quantum-resistant algorithms and updating existing infrastructure to accommodate these changes. The transition necessitates a long-term planning and investment, ensuring a smooth migration without compromising current security. This transition should be a gradual, well-planned evolution, taking into consideration various factors and potential challenges. A proactive approach is needed to remain secure in the quantum computing era.

7.3 Security Threats and Mitigation

API gateways, while offering robust security features, aren't impervious to threats. A common vulnerability lies in insufficient input validation. Attackers might exploit weaknesses by injecting malicious code or data, leading to vulnerabilities like SQL injection or cross-site scripting (XSS). Implementing strict input validation, sanitizing all data before processing, and utilizing parameterized queries in database interactions are crucial mitigation strategies. Regular security audits and penetration testing can proactively identify and address such vulnerabilities before they're exploited. Remember, a layered security approach is always best.

Another significant threat stems from insufficient API key management. Weak or easily guessable API keys can grant unauthorized access to your microservices. Employ strong key generation practices, including using random and sufficiently long keys. Regular key rotation and revocation mechanisms are essential, limiting the impact of compromised keys. Consider utilizing key management systems (KMS) that provide robust key lifecycle management capabilities, enhancing overall security posture. These systems often offer features like encryption and access control, significantly reducing the risks.

Denial-of-service (DoS) attacks remain a constant threat. These attacks aim to overwhelm your API gateway, making it unavailable to legitimate users. Employ rate limiting and throttling mechanisms to restrict the number of requests from a single IP address or user within a specific time frame. Implementing robust caching strategies can also help absorb some attack traffic. Moreover, consider deploying distributed denial-of-service (DDoS) mitigation solutions, often provided by cloud providers or specialized security vendors. These solutions can effectively absorb and filter malicious traffic, protecting your API gateway's availability.

Security headers are often overlooked yet are vital in bolstering your API gateway's security. Headers like HTTP Strict Transport Security (HSTS) enforce HTTPS connections, preventing man-in-the-middle attacks. Content Security Policy (CSP) headers control the resources your API allows to load, limiting the impact of XSS attacks. X-Frame-Options prevents clickjacking, another form of attack. Correctly configuring these headers adds a significant layer of defense against various common attacks. Detailed documentation and understanding are crucial, ensuring proper implementation tailored to your specific environment.

The security of your underlying infrastructure is paramount. Vulnerabilities in your servers, databases, or network devices can expose your API gateway to attacks. Regular patching and updates, along with robust intrusion detection and prevention systems (IDPS), are crucial elements of a holistic security strategy. Consider using hardened server configurations, minimizing attack surfaces by disabling unnecessary services and ports. A proactive approach to infrastructure security significantly strengthens the overall protection of your API gateway.

Finally, don't underestimate the importance of monitoring and logging. Comprehensive logging provides valuable insights into API usage patterns, helping detect anomalies and potential attacks. Real-time monitoring of your API gateway's performance and security metrics enables prompt responses to security incidents. Effective alerting systems notify your security team of suspicious activities, allowing for immediate intervention and mitigation. Regular review of logs and security alerts is essential, assisting in identifying emerging threats and adapting your security posture accordingly. Remember, proactive threat detection and timely response can mitigate risks effectively. This requires meticulous attention to detail and a continuous improvement mindset in the realm of API security. Integrating security deeply into the development lifecycle, incorporating security assessments, and promoting a culture of security awareness within your team are crucial for long-term success.

7.4 The Future of API Security

The landscape of API security is constantly evolving, demanding a proactive and adaptable approach. We've already covered the fundamentals; now, let's look ahead. Expect increasingly sophisticated attacks targeting vulnerabilities in API design and implementation. Zero-trust architectures, once a niche concept, will become the standard, demanding rigorous verification at every access point. This means moving beyond simple authentication and embracing robust authorization models, granularly controlling access based on context and user roles. This shift will require significant changes in how we design and manage APIs. Think about implementing fine-grained authorization policies, going beyond simple role-based access control to context-aware access control. This ensures that only authorized users can access specific data and functionalities, even if they possess broader access privileges. The adoption of this approach will drastically reduce the attack surface and enhance the overall security posture of your API ecosystem.

Beyond the traditional perimeter security model, the future of API security leans heavily on AI-driven threat detection and response. Machine learning algorithms, trained on vast datasets of API traffic and attack patterns, will play a crucial role in identifying and mitigating threats in real-time. This will empower organizations to respond to threats quickly and efficiently, reducing the impact of potential breaches and minimizing downtime. Moreover, continuous monitoring and automated remediation will be key, using AI-powered tools that analyze API traffic, identifying anomalies, and automatically taking corrective actions, such as blocking malicious requests or temporarily disabling compromised APIs. These automated responses provide an immediate safety net to any potential breach, giving you a level of protection that constant manual monitoring can't match.

The rise of serverless computing further complicates API security. With functions deployed on demand, traditional security models become insufficient. Serverless architectures necessitate a shift towards function-level security, where access control and authorization are implemented at the individual function level, rather than just at the API gateway level. Implementing a micro-segmentation strategy is crucial for limiting the potential damage of a breach and enhancing overall resilience. This involves dividing your serverless infrastructure into smaller, isolated segments, ensuring that even if one segment is compromised, the attacker can't easily spread laterally throughout your system. This architectural paradigm will improve the overall security and resilience of your API systems, enabling agile and secure deployment of your functions in the cloud.

Furthermore, the integration of blockchain technology presents both opportunities and challenges. Blockchain's immutability can enhance the security and transparency of API transactions, providing an audit trail that is difficult to tamper with. However, securing blockchain-based APIs requires specialized knowledge and tools, as traditional security measures may not be sufficient. The secure implementation of blockchain-based APIs requires careful consideration of cryptographic techniques and secure key management protocols. Ensuring the integrity and confidentiality of data stored on the blockchain demands adopting rigorous access control measures and encrypting sensitive information. It's equally important to regularly update security patches, conduct penetration testing, and implement robust security monitoring mechanisms to detect and respond to threats promptly.

Finally, the human element remains a critical vulnerability. Robust security training programs for developers and API administrators are paramount. This isn't just about technical skills, but also about fostering a security-conscious culture. Regular security awareness training should be implemented, and this training should cover topics such as secure coding practices, understanding common API vulnerabilities, and recognizing social engineering tactics. Implementing a robust bug bounty program can incentivize the discovery and reporting of security vulnerabilities, which helps organizations identify and fix issues quickly. It will also encourage collaboration between security professionals and developers, promoting a shared responsibility for ensuring the overall security of the API infrastructure. Investing in continuous training, frequent security audits, and building a proactive security culture is vital in creating resilient API environments for the future. Remember, the strongest technology is useless without responsible human operators.

7.5 Conclusion

Our journey through the intricacies of API gateways and authentication gatekeepers concludes here. We've traversed the landscape of security protocols, explored best practices, and delved into the practical implementation of securing microservices. Remember the fundamental importance of choosing the right API gateway for your specific needs, considering factors like scalability, security features, and ease of integration with existing infrastructure. The wrong choice can significantly hinder your project's success. The process, while demanding, is ultimately rewarding; a secure and efficient system significantly reduces vulnerabilities and ensures smooth operation.

Careful planning and meticulous execution are paramount. Don't underestimate the power of thorough testing throughout the development lifecycle. Regular penetration testing and security audits are not merely optional; they're indispensable components of a robust security posture. These processes identify weaknesses before malicious actors exploit them, ensuring a resilient system capable of withstanding various attacks. Ignoring these crucial steps leaves your system vulnerable and exposed to potentially devastating consequences. Proactive security measures are far more effective and cost-efficient than reactive damage control.

Moreover, consider the human element. Security awareness training for your development team is absolutely crucial. Educating your team about common vulnerabilities, secure coding practices, and the importance of following security best practices significantly reduces the risk of introducing security flaws during development. Regular training and updates ensure that your team stays informed about emerging threats and effective mitigation strategies. This investment in human capital significantly improves the overall security posture of your system.

The ongoing evolution of technology necessitates a commitment to continuous learning and adaptation. The cybersecurity landscape is constantly shifting, with new threats emerging regularly. Staying abreast of the latest security trends, vulnerabilities, and best practices is essential for maintaining a robust security posture. This requires ongoing monitoring of security news, participation in relevant communities, and regular updates to your security protocols and technologies. Remember, complacency is the enemy of security.

Finally, remember the broader context. Security isn't an isolated concern; it's interwoven with other aspects of system design, including performance, scalability, and maintainability. A secure system that's slow, difficult to maintain, or doesn't scale effectively ultimately fails to fulfill its purpose. Strive for a balanced approach that prioritizes security without sacrificing other critical aspects of your application's functionality and usability. The ideal system is both secure and efficient, meeting the needs of both developers and users. Strive for that balance. A successful implementation represents a significant achievement, one that safeguards valuable data and ensures the smooth functioning of your entire system. Embrace the challenges, learn from your experiences, and continuously improve your approach to API security.

www.ingramcontent.com/pod-product-compliance
Lightning Source LLC
LaVergne TN
LVHW022021200926
848481LV00007B/2472

* 9 7 9 8 3 4 8 5 2 4 9 2 0 *